# THE
# WONDER
# OF
# BEING
# LOVED

# THE WONDER OF BEING LOVED

**MESSAGES FOR LENT AND EVERY SEASON**

**ALVIN N. ROGNESS**

**AUGSBURG PUBLISHING HOUSE**
Minneapolis, Minnesota

THE WONDER OF BEING LOVED

Manufactured in the United States of America

# Contents

Preface ........................................................................... 7

1. How It All Began ................................................. 9

2. The Big Family ..................................................... 17

3. The Risk We Take ................................................ 25

4. The Shattered Walls ............................................ 35

5. The Genius of Forgiveness ................................. 45

6. The Recovery of Hope ........................................ 55

7. A Style of Life ..................................................... 65

# Preface

The chapters of this book are the refinement of sermons given at First Lutheran Church, Sioux Falls, South Dakota, on Wednesday evenings during Lent on the occasion of the 50th anniversary of the congregation.

The title, *The Wonder of Being Loved,* expresses the dominant theme of Lent. Nothing but the radical and glorious love of God for man can do justice to the recurring message of Lent in the church's year.

To declare this love, with the cross as the mysterious focus of its revelation to man, is the central task of the church not only during Lent, but the year around. Each of these messages is intended to impress the reader not only with the wonder of being loved, but also with the peril and the glory that such love entails.

I express gratitude to First Lutheran Church for the invitation to give these sermons, but far more for its having been my church home during my college years and later for having honored me by calling me as its pastor. To its members and to its pastor for a third of a century, H. J. Glenn, I owe more than I can know.

ALVIN N. ROGNESS

7

# How It All Began

*When in former times God spoke to our forefathers, he spoke in fragmentary and varied fashion through the prophets. But in this final age he has spoken to us in the Son whom he has made heir to the whole universe.*

Hebrews 1:1-2 (NEB)

# 1.

A congregation is no ordinary grouping of people. It has its beginnings far back in the heart of God. He created them in love, and he can not let them go. This was his trouble, and this is our glory. We are attached to him, not by dint of our own will nor by the excellence of our performance. We are the created ones, the redeemed ones, the called ones, the gathered ones. We are the people being reshaped into the beings he intended us to be from the beginning. Through Word and Sacrament the Holy Spirit broods over us, penetrates us, disturbs us, condemns us—and then captures us by the incredible love revealed in Christ Jesus. Little wonder that we are, deep down, a peculiar people.

A congregation may seem very much like any other organization made up of all kinds of people. They are of many occupations. They have widely different tastes in music, art, and fashion. They have varied political and economic views. And they have all the weaknesses that plague the human race—prejudice, hatred, indifference, fear, even despair. But these are the kinds of people Jesus Christ came to call. It was for this sort he died. Theirs are the ills the Holy Spirit is at work to change.

One might wonder if God thinks it all worth while. The change in people is often not spectacular enough to create any rhapsody. Read the Old Testament to catch some of the pathos of God. He had chosen a people to be his own. Time and again, they turned from him. It is a wonder that his patience held out. Why did he not let them go, once and for all? But he did not. He was "stuck" with them—because he could not stop loving them. He kept on their trail through the prophets, a long line of them. Finally, he sent his only Son. This was and is the measure of his love.

These two thousand years, since the coming of our Lord and the establishing of his kingdom on earth, have not been an epic of unabridged glory for the church. It will take more than a casual analysis to discover the glory of God in the people of God. We fail him again and again, in every generation. But we are nonetheless a peculiar people. The love of God in Christ has touched us. And we are never again the same. Within our hearts, deep within, something is at work. The kingdom is within us and in our midst, even if neat, discernible criteria may not be found to pinpoint its presence. We live by faith, and the works of God can often be seen only with the eyes of faith.

The church is under severe judgment today. The judgment is leveled by the church itself, against itself. Sometimes it seems almost cruel, as if a person is lashing himself in a fury of masochism. But we need not defend ourselves. If we come together in the Spirit of our Lord at all, we will come in repentence. We must confess that we have failed our Lord and our neighbor in a hundred different ways. Our only cry to God is for mercy.

The church may indeed be on trial. But not the Lord of the church. It is not he that has failed. It is precisely at this point that we need to be vigilant. The age attempts to put God himself on trial. We are bedeviled by enormous problems. There is the bomb, overpopulation, hunger, injustice, crime, drugs, violence. Voices cry, "Why doesn't God *do* something? If he cannot or will not, let him step aside. He must be relevant, or we won't have him. The world is aflame, and if he cannot man the hoses to put out the fires, let him sit it out on the curb until we have the blaze under control. Then we may have the leisure to go back to him." What insane effrontery! Who are we to put God on trial? If there is a God at all, it is he who does the judging.

Let us remember that God is pictured as a great and good Father. When his children mismanage their lives and the planet, he has three options. He can let us go our wayward ways, be through with us, and have us mess up the planet in any way we choose. But he does not let us go. Or, he can take over the management, discharge us from having dominion of this earth, deny us any decision-making, reduce us to puppets and have us, like automatons, do only that which he wanted us to do. He can demote us to the decision-less life of the winds that blow or the rain that falls. But he does not.

Instead he has given us the gift of choice, and even if we use the gift to navigate ourselves and the planet to hell and eternal separation, he will not withdraw the gift. He chose to ride it out with us, even when it cost him his own life on a cross.

It is this story that defines the mission of the church. Everything it does is focused on the telling and doing of that story. And what a story it is, from the very first verse in Genesis to the last verse of the Book of Revelation. There is nothing like it in all the literature of the world. In fact, it must be the Word of God, his revelation, because for sheer audacity in its claims for man, it has no parallel. What diseased imagination could conceive that the God who created and manages this vast universe could bother with this tiny planet and these disappointing creatures that keep despoiling it? No writer of fiction in his right mind could hatch such a plot.

The Almighty God chose you and me to be like him, to live with him, to make common cause with him, and to be as his sons. And when in disobedience and selfishness we turned our backs on him, abandoned him and arrayed ourselves against him, he went the lengths of a cross to recover us. And he has a place for us back in his enterprises, if we will. Back with him, however badly we function, he continues to forgive and restore.

There simply is no story in all the world like it. And

the church has been chosen to tell it. Everything else the church may do revolves around it, departs from it, returns to it, lives within it. It is the gospel and it has the power to make everything new.

In response to a God like this, what does man do? Thank him? Yes, indeed. And praise him? Of course. When we ask what is the ultimate purpose for man upon the earth, the church has for centuries had one comprehensive and simple answer: to glorify God and to serve him and enjoy him forever. It is not enough just to survive. Nor to achieve more pleasure than pain these few, swift years. Nor even to make the world a better place. There is a bigger reason for living. Come what may, whether our days be short or long, whether we prosper or fail, whether the world blows up or not, we have one overarching purpose—to glorify God, to serve him and to enjoy him.

At first sight, this may seem an impractical answer. How about serving governments, industries, the arts and the sciences? These are objectives near at hand. God is someone we have never seen or touched or heard. How can anyone serve him and be involved in the hard, concrete situations of our day by day living? Jesus said, "Seek ye first the kingdom of God and his righteousness, and all these things shall be added to you," and we might very well add, "including relevance." For in the final analysis, life on this earth will depend more on man's loyalty to God than on anything else.

History is replete with people who did take God seriously, and who in consequence took more seriously the causes of justice and mercy in government, in education, in industry. They became fiercely relevant.

If it were possible to document the inner motives of men, I think it might very well be demonstrated that no significant advance in human welfare and human rights has been made in our Western world except through the agency or influence of some person or persons who have had a profound encounter with God and who have turned to thank God by serving their fellowmen.

When the kind of love Christ has had for us, and still has, breaks in upon the heart of a man, something happens to him. He turns to his brother in a new way. He sets out to return God's love to him by passing it on to the brother. He asks only "Does my brother have needs?" He does not even ask if he likes his brother. Like him or not, he has no choice but to be concerned with him. It is the only option God opens to him. How can he demonstrate his love and concern for God except in the language of concern for the brother?

# The Big Family

*I bow my knees before the Father, from whom every family in heaven and on earth is named, that according to the riches of his glory he may grant you to be strengthened with might through his Spirit in the inner man, and that Christ may dwell in your hearts through faith.*

Ephesians 3:14-17 (RSV)

## 2.

There is a given solidarity about the human family. They are one! Their solidarity lies not in their similarities. At least, not primarily so. Every normal human being, despite his color or creed, does have two legs, two arms, two eyes, one heart. In chemical composition they analyze out to the same basic elements.

But the oneness of the human family stems basically from the fact that all are intended to be sons of God. They have a given worth and dignity. Whether bushmen or doctors of philosophy, they are God's children. We are a big family, of almost infinite variety, but one family nonetheless. No brother has a right to disdain a brother.

The Bible makes it very clear, however, that a man may leave the family, may drift into a far country and may be eternally lost to the Father. Or, that for want of knowing that he belongs to the Father he may miss altogether the riches of the Father's house and life. Every church's task therefore is primarily to call the children back home to the Father. If a church fails in this one, towering commission, it forfeits its life. It then has no more uniqueness than a thousand other human groupings.

Those of us who have heard the call of God, have reentered the Father's house, and are at work there must remember that we have no more claim to the Father's love than those who are on the outside. Nor are we necessarily of greater virtue. Some other grouping of men who do not confess God at all may at times evidence more love, more patience, and more concern than a church. This should not be, of course, and it is to the shame of a people who are aware of the love of God.

For us to be at all priggish about being Christian is to deny the love of God itself. To become a cozy group, reveling in the fact that we have been reclaimed by God, smug over being the ingroup, condescending or patronizing toward our brothers on the outside—this is to emasculate our witness altogether. The man on the outside is worth as much as the man on the inside. In the parable of the Prodigal Son, the father loved his son as much when he was estranged from him in the far country as when he was at home. And he was a son, whether at home or away from home. When he returned you may remember, the father prepared a great feast and invited all his neighbors saying, "My son who was dead is alive; my son who was lost is found." A person may be a lost son or a found son, a dead son or a live son, but a son nonetheless. In that context, every human being is a son of God.

It is one of the puzzles of the age that man, who has achieved so much in the discovery and control of his universe, should at this very moment sell himself so short. We have very little confidence in ourselves. We tremble at the forces that threaten to destroy us. The bravado which was ours in the first part of this century is gone. We had naively believed that the world was growing better, day by day and year by year. We boasted that "the kingdom of God" was just around the corner. We had climbed the high mountains, had left behind us the brutish ways of the past, and were about to emerge into a self-made utopia.

Suddenly optimism is gone. We see mankind's tenure on the planet almost ended. We will be blown off by our bombs or we will choke to death in widespread emphysema. Meanwhile, in extensive self-analysis by biochemists, psychologist, and social scientists, we have reduced ourselves to some blobs of complex protoplasm. We surrender any claim to self-determination by yielding to the fact that environment, heredity, and biochemistry jointly determine everything we do. We join the large family of amoebas, chimpanzees, white rats, and guinea pigs. We become little more than the chemical elements of a test tube.

It is the tragedy of our century that vast numbers of God's children deliberately surrender the only valid claim they have to dignity and worth. We are all members of the most royal family in the universe. We are sons and daughters, princes and princesses, in God's family, under orders to manage this planet for him and destined after death to live with him forever. Is there anything in all the world to give man dignity compared with this?

This dignity is not altered by man's mismanagement. If men turn to alcohol, drug addiction, and fornication, they do so as children of God. If they forget all the policies of God and plunge on in an insane pursuit of profit, power, or pleasure, they are still a royal company. Rebelling against God, they are still sons. When Absalom rebelled against his father, King David, he was still a son. The very fact that he was a son made his rebellion the more tragic. If it had been a peasant that rebelled, it would have been but an incident. But it was a son. And his rebellion shook the kingdom and broke the king's heart.

Our age would be vastly helped by understanding that our mismanagement of the planet is more serious than survival itself. After all, we have faced individual death throughout the ages. This is nothing new. Is it much different to face the death of the planet itself? To lengthen the span of life is not the ultimate issue. To achieve a quality of life, to be aware of the worth and dignity of a human being, no matter how long or short his life—this has always been the issue for noble and reflective people. Such awareness obviously will have a bearing on the survival of the planet. But here is the issue: is man a child of God, at work in the Father's house and within the policies of the Father's kingdom, come what may?

To this question the church, and the church alone, has the grand answer. There is no other institution in society that can supply this dimension of life. And without this dimension, it is highly questionable whether man can marshall either the will or the wisdom to manage this planet, even for its survival. With it, the future is as open and unpredictable as the power of God itself.

If the church is to supply this exalted view of man and really communicate it to our generation, it will need to be reminded constantly of the central tenets of its own faith.

It will need to understand the glorious impartiality of the Father. He lets his sun shine on the good and the evil, his rain fall on the just and the unjust. He loves all his children equally, whether they betray him or not. There are no favorites. Even the "chosen people" of the Old Testament were not favorites. They were chosen for a special function. But they were not the elite. All people are the elite, sons and daughters of the great God.

It will need to find its own identity in the sheer mercy of God. The cardinal creed of our faith is the justification of the sinner by grace through faith. We have no other credential for our life nor for our mission than that. We are sons of God through the unmerited favor of God himself, in the life and work of our mediator and redeemer, Jesus Christ. He became our brother, through love, identified with our fallen plight, took on our sins, went to a cross to settle the accounts of sin once and for all, and threw wide the door to the Father's house for our return. Whatever righteousness we may have is a given righteousness. We cannot strut in it; we can only thank for it. We have become a church of Jesus Christ through forgiveness, and we live constantly in the cradle of that forgiveness. We continue to have one prayer, "God be merciful to me, a sinner."

It will turn to those outside of the church, not as "the haves" over against "the have-nots" but as beggars still, inviting other beggars to the feast. This is the clue to all evangelism

We live in a day when the universality of *the human* is growing spectacularly. We are one world. We are one human family. The superb statement on Human Rights adopted by the United Nations is evidence that all nations are recognizing that no people on the earth has a right to be the aristocrats. Hitler's premise that the Anglo-Saxons were destined to rule the world is gone. Even the North Atlantic world, the Western world, knows now that the ancient cultures of Asia and Africa have been given values of universal worth that ought not necessarily be replaced by those of the Western white race. We are on the threshold of a day when all people everywhere will stand in respect and even awe over against the worth and the rights of all other people.

It is a most auspicious day for the church of the Bible.

Throughout its 66 books, if we will read them aright, there is enforced upon us the glorious fact that "all people have been created in the image of God." All people of all places and stations are enfolded in the love of this God. The maimed, the blind, the retarded, the insane, the criminals—all are endowed by their Creator and Redeemer with the rights to the Father's limitless kingdom. The pigmies and the bushmen join with Beethoven and Socrates in this exalted company.

The church has the high privilege and the solemn duty to bring this perspective. This is the anthropology to tower over all other views of man. It is the assessment of man that eventually may modify the foreign policies of nations. It is the point of view that can forever outlaw genocide, hunger, and war. No child of God has a right within the Father's family to treat any other child with anything less than the dignity given by God to angels and to men!

# The Risk We Take

*Where the Spirit of the Lord is, there is freedom. And we all, with unveiled face, beholding the glory of the Lord, are being changed into his likeness from one degree of glory to another.*

2 Corinthians 3:17-18 (RSV)

# 3.

What can you lose? You have everything to gain in belonging to the church. Most respected and successful people belong; to know them may in fact help you get on in life. You will be asked for some support, to be sure, but really only a modest part of your income. You will be asked to believe in God, of course. But again, what can you lose? If there is no God, your gamble has cost you little. And if there is a God, you've got heaven to gain. Unfortunately, too many people probably are just such kind of members.

But they are in danger, great danger. They come within God's magnetic field. In Word and Sacraments the Holy Spirit broods and roams and strikes. At some unsuspecting moment the Spirit may break through a man's casual and cautious crust. Things will never be the same for him again. All heaven may burst in upon him.

If a man is content to remain as he is, he should never darken the doors of a church. Jesus Christ is lord here. His ways are as terrifying as they are glorious. And he has a plot—to have every person become like him.

And the church works with and through a frightening book. The ancient Norsemen had a legend about a "Black Book," its pages black and its print in red blood.

It was the book of the devil. Anyone who opened the book would become possessed, in the grip of Satan. The Bible is God's book, its pages surging with the story of God. Lurking within its pages is the Spirit of God, waiting and hoping to possess its readers. Even the casual reader may be caught. Like a fisherman throwing his line to catch a fish and suddenly finding himself drawn into the waters by the big fish that strikes—so the "objective" reader of this book may unsuspectingly be drawn into the deep and be possessed of God.

The kingdom of God is like that. Throughout the centuries it has drawn into its borders millions of people who never again had their lives in the commonplaces. They became disciples or followers of Jesus. Think what it cost Peter to drop his fishing and tag along with Jesus. Step by step he was drawn deeper into the life-style of Jesus, until he could not possibly extricate himself. Legend has it that when, after Christ's resurrection and ascension, he was the leader of the disciples in Rome, one day in fear of persecution and death he fled from the city. Walking on the road, suddenly he was face to face with Jesus. Peter asked, "Where are you going, Lord?" Jesus answered, "I go to Rome to be crucified." The vision gone, Peter turned to reenter Rome and finally to be crucified for his faith—but crucified head down at his request, as not worthy to be crucified in the same manner as his Lord.

In many less dramatic ways, lives have been set on

new paths of love and service. It is a dangerous thing to come within reach of Jesus Christ.

You cannot face him without facing yourself. And if you face yourself against the purity and love of this person, your entire inventory of self-esteem is shattered. Every excuse for shabby performance dies on your lips, every fragment of self-pity fades away. Every inclination to self-indulgence becomes fraudulent. Your defenses are totally broken. You stand before him stripped. You have no cry but for mercy.

> Upon the cross of Jesus
> Mine eyes at times can see
> The very dying form of one
> Who suffered there for me.
> And from my smitten heart
> Two wonders I confess,
> The wonder of his glorious love
> And my unworthiness.

Within the church, in symbol, in music, in preaching, in the sacraments, you come full into the face of the cross. It will haunt you. You may steel yourself against it, but it is there to pursue you. And if the Holy Spirit has his way with you, you will cry out in your heart, "What must I do?" You cannot let Christ and his cross go without a response. You can reject them.

If you do, you betray him who loves you with an everlasting love, you betray yourself, you betray your brothers, and you are doomed to a life in the shallows, wallowing in the mire of self. You let go the divine; you are denied the essentially human.

When I understand the full implications of Christ's love, I can very well pause before I yield to him. It would be tragic, but by commonly accepted standards of caution, it would not seem strange. Suppose a young Caesar were to fall madly in love with a palace maid and ask her to become his wife, the queen of the empire. The maid would be overwhelmed with the prospect of such honor and station—perhaps also terrified at the passion of his love. What should she do? The fact was that all she wanted was to return to Milan, her home, and marry a school teacher—and that's what she did. Comprehending the majestic role Christ has in store for me, I may decline the honor. But it will be at dear cost. I will have missed the very purpose for my life these swift years. I was not created to marry the Milan schoolmaster; I was created to live and work with God.

It is the very passion of Christ's love that threatens to overwhelm us. It is more than and different from human love. It is the *agape* of God. It is the kind of love you cannot stop. Nothing you do will stop God from loving you. Human love is different. It is human, and natural, for us to love the lovely, to be attracted to the attractive. It is divine to love the unlovely and be attracted to the unattractive. God's love is like that. He loves the unlovely and unloving, and by the sheer power of his love transforms the ugly to the lovely.

It is human, and natural, to love someone, to lavish concern on him, because of his possibilities. A teacher may have a boy in her class, the most incorrigible of the lot, in whom she sees real possibilities. She lavishes her affection and concern on him, month after month. If, however, after a year or more of this he remains as impudent and irritating as ever, she may very well wash her hands of him and regret ever having done anything for him. God's concern is different. If he should have loved mankind for their possibilities, how long since would he not have given up on us?

God loves us because it is his nature to love. Year in and year out, he continues to love. We cannot stop him, any more than we can stop the sun from shining. We can draw the blinds and stop the sun's rays from reaching us. We can turn our backs on God and renounce his love. We can live as if he did not exist. But we cannot stop him from loving us.

It is this kind of love he wants to give us, and to have possess us. He wants to unloose on this earth, through us, a veritable tide of this kind of love. We then will love others *as* we have been loved by God, and *because* we are loved by God. We will love people, not because we are attracted to them, not because we like them. There may be all sorts of things we do not like about them. In fact, there are many things I don't like about myself. But this does not stop me from a deep concern for myself. Love your neighbor as yourself, said Jesus. Caught by the love of God, I turn to my unattractive, unlovely but needy neighbor to sweep him into the orbit of my deep concern.

Moreover, I do not love the neighbor for what he may become. I love him as he is, and will continue to love him, even if none of my hopes for him materialize. I love him, even if he spurns my love, rejects me, and lashes out at me.

A man in the high echelons of government told me that when he tried to do good to people and they turned against him, or when the odds of achieving anything seemed insuperable, then he would stop trying—if he were not under higher orders. But he was a follower of him who loved and loved, who tried and tried, unrelenting. And he could not quit. He had to keep on. For he was a disciple, a member indeed of the great church of Jesus Christ.

It would be a betrayal of the gospel if we did not also speak of the incomparable comfort we can know as we nestle in the love of God. William James in his *Varieties of Religious Experience* speaks of the "Gospel of Relaxation." We have great need of resting back in the everlasting arms. In our day especially, when the church is reminded repeatedly of what it has not done and what it ought to be doing, we have a right to be reminded that it is God who carries us and not we who carry God. We are children, after all, and we need to be enfolded in the love and strength of a heavenly Father.

Sidney Lanier in "The Marshes of Glynn" says, "As the marsh-hen secretly builds on the watery sod, Behold I will build me a nest on the greatness of God." My continuing comfort will be the assurance that I am the loved one, the forgiven one—that nothing shall be able to separate me from the love of God in Jesus Christ.

It is only when I am overwhelmed by being loved by this great Somebody that I too become a somebody. I am important, precisely because I already am the chosen one, the loved one. And because I am loved, the need to be a rival and competitor of my brother disappears. I need no further guarantee for status. I am loved, and can afford to cease all rivalries for acclaim, and can turn in freedom to be a brother in love to all men.

I have known people like that, and so have you. They are not sensitive to honors or station. They swing free from all pettiness or peevishness. They take no notice when you forget to thank them. They have hardly any self-consciousness; they are absorbed in the needs and joys of others. They make great companions on a fishing trip. They are the kind of people you hope your son or daughter might marry.

They were not born this way. They are products, at least in part, of the ministry of the gospel. They have come faithfully, Sunday after Sunday, within earshot of the Word of God. They are the creations of the Spirit of God. They have come, they have taken the great risk, and they are emissaries of the love of God in this world.

# The Shattered Walls

*"Compel people to come in."*

Luke 14:23 **(RSV)**

*"The kingdom of heaven is like leaven which a woman took and hid in three measures of meal, till it was all leavened."*

Matthew 13:33 (RSV)

# 4.

The church has two mandates. It is to bring the world into the church, and it is to bring the church into the world. It gathers and it scatters. It is a rendezvous with God; it is an army in battle for God. It is not of the world, but it is in the world.

It has three strategies over against its world: it *evangelizes,* it *infiltrates,* it *confronts.*

Christ's last recorded command (Matthew 28) is that we go into the world and make disciples. We are to win followers for Jesus. We are to bring them *in*— into the fellowship of the believers, the church. We bring to the world the great story, the gospel. We evangelize.

In a singular sense this commission is the unique one. The early followers of Jesus expected his imminent return. They had no illusion about changing the world. They set out to rescue people from the world which they expected soon to end. There is no talk in the New Testament about staging a religious revival in order to brace up the tottering Greco-Roman civilization. They did not set out to infiltrate the culture. They set out to win souls for an eternal kingdom.

Almost at once the little band of disciples began to fan out into the world. They began at Jerusalem, then Judea, then Samaria, and in wider and wider concentric circles into all the world. Before the century was over they were in Rome, in Spain, in North Africa. They recognized that the world was their field. They could have formed a little club of Jesus-followers in Jerusalem. But they were restless with the Lord's command. He had given them a world for a field.

Any true congregation senses this same urgency. It cannot minister only to itself. It must reach out. It has no option. It is a missionary congregation. It comes to its task with one, towering tool. It has a gospel to proclaim and to minister. Its Lord staked everything on winning a world by the telling of a story. If this failed, he had no alternative to offer.

And what a story it is! It tells of God and of man, and God's way with man. God created man in his image, in his likeness. He gave to him alone, among all his earthly creatures, the gift of choice. Man could transcend his environment and heredity, in part at least defy them, and could make decisions and follow a course of action which was his own. The story goes on to describe man's perfidy, how he used this gift to disobey God, to be led into captivity by the enemy of God. But this is not the end. God put into action a plan to recover man, and in the fullness of time sent his only Son, Jesus Christ, to invade the earth, overcome the enemy, break down the doors of the enemy's prison, fling wide the doors of the Father's house, overcome death, provide forgiveness for the sins of men, and give them title to the eternal kingdom again.

The story puts God definitely on the side of life, abundant life for his children. It was not his will that there should be sin, tragedy, pain, and death. These were intruders, which came in through the back door in the wake of man's disobedience. God's entire action, from beginning to end, is to restore to man the dignity and the destiny which he had planned when he created him.

The stupendous motif in this story is the love of God. Everything he does for and with man speaks of a love that will not let him go. Because he loves man so, he suffers with him and for him. The cross is the supreme symbol. "Greater love has no man than this, that a man lay down his life for his friends . . . you are my friends."

This is the story. And when the church tells it faithfully and in its life reflects this love of God, then people are shaken to the depths. They cry, "What language shall I borrow, to thank thee, dearest friend?" And the language which the Lord himself provides is the language of service, a service in love to God and to all men everywhere. The church has this distinctive mission above all others: to tell the story which has the power to enlist followers, responsible disciples. This is the incomparable gift it has to bring to the world.

While its avowed and open mission is to evangelize the world, it also has the subtle but powerful role of *infiltrating* the world. It is a leaven, a yeast, a salt, touching every area of the world's life.

The gospel converts people, and through converted people it penetrates all the orders of creation—the family, governments, education, industry, communication, labor, science, the arts

Nor is this only a derivative function of the church. After all, when God created man he gave him dominion over this earth. We were to manage it for him. The earth is the Lord's, every square inch of it. He never gave it over to Satan. Much harm has inadvertently been done by relegating God to heaven and leaving the earth to fend for itself. He is interested not only in the souls of men and the eventual heavenly tenure for man. He created both body and soul, the whole man. God has a profound concern that the kingdom may come to us and we to the kingdom, here and now.

He knows, and we know, that only on the other side of death can he make perfect that which he began at creation. The forces of evil are yet deeply entrenched in the human heart and in the affairs of earth, despite the fact that the kingdom of our Lord has already been established among us. Why God does not end this regime, where wars and disease can distort and damage the life of his children—this we cannot know. One day, upon his return, the Lord will end it. In the meantime, we have the high privilege of being his ambassadors, his managers in all the enterprises of this world's life.

What immeasurable good has come to the world through the instruments of men and women who have taken seriously the Lord's will for their lives only God can assess. Think of the people in government and in industry who have had integrity and mercy and who have discharged their day-by-day responsibilities as followers of their Lord. They are the unseen leaven. They are the salt that keeps society from rotting. They are the adhesive that holds the structures of life together.

The story is told of Sir William Wilberforce, who as a young member of the British Parliament had a decisive encounter with God. For a time he thought to surrender his seat in Parliament and go into "religious" work. His friend, the younger Pitt, dissuaded him and convinced him to give his life in a fight against the cancer of the Empire, the legalized slave traffic. Years later, Parliament met one evening to vote out the traffic once and for all. It was reported that the principal speaker ended his remarks with these words: "I am thinking tonight of two heads and two pillows. One is the head of Napoleon, tossing feverishly on a pillow on the island of Helena, after having left a trail of blood from Jena to Waterloo. One is the man who tonight will see the consummation of his life's work. If I were to choose, I would not choose the pillow of Napoleon. I would choose the head that will rest tonight, after our vote is taken, on the pillow of Wilberforce."

All through the ages, in small instances and in large, men and women whose lives have been captured by the Lord have been this kind of leaven in society. They have turned to their brothers, in the structures of government and industry, to discharge their gratitude for God's great mercy by noble service to this earth.

When in our day the church is charged with indifference to the plight of the poor and the disfranchised of the earth, in all fairness we need to remember that the ways of the kingdom are not always the stuff that breaks into print. We need to remember that in countless quiet and unnoticed ways the gospel has reshaped people, events, and structures. The kingdom of God is a leaven. It infiltrates!

There are doubtless times when the church, as an organized, visible body, must *confront* its world. With prophetic clarity, it must call the age to justice and mercy. As an organization, it is a focus of power, and there may be times when it must use this power to confront other centers of power.

This confrontation faces some difficult problems. In the first place, we must ask, "Who and what is the church?" Is the church the bishop, a majority of the members, a council of elected leaders, or the unanimous voice of all its members? After all, the church is made up of people who in faith receive the Lord, Jesus Christ, as their Lord and Savior. Beyond that, what can we say? Loyal to their Lord and seeking his will, they may—and indeed must—agree in broad, general principles. They must be for justice and mercy; they must be against untruth, cruelty, oppression, destructive pleasures. But in the concrete issues relating to how justice and freedom are best to be achieved, they may differ widely. Most of the choices we are forced to make in this world are choices between a greater and a lesser evil. We struggle in gray areas, each follower of Jesus seeking the course his conscience must take.

Some decades ago many churches took an open stand for what became the Volstead Act, a total prohibition of any traffic in alcoholic beverages. Many sincere Christians were convinced that this was not the best way to curb the evils of alcohol. Did "the church" have a right to speak for them, and indeed was it "the church" that had spoken?

In our day there is a great clamor for the church to become bold and speak out on the issues of the day. It may very well be that some issues have surfaced clearly enough for the church, as a corporate voice, to speak without equivocation. And we may very well ask if the church is not indeed doing so. Are not a great chorus of the voices raised in protest to nuclear war, pollution, injustice for minorities, and traffic in drugs and alcohol coming from people whom the church has sensitized in conscience?

We need not come to the defense of the organized church. It would be quite inappropriate for us to do so. We have fallen far short. Our indifference to the ills of our fellowmen cries to heaven. We need to repent and cry for mercy. We need to seek our Lord's will in our day, and pray for the will to follow him, whatever it may cost.

But we must not forget that the Lord himself, in his own way of life on earth, has pointed his church to evangelization and infiltration as the unique mission for its life on the earth.

# The Genius of Forgiveness

*In him we have redemption through his blood, the forgiveness of our trespasses, according to the riches of his grace.*

Ephesians 1:7 (RSV)

*Where there is forgiveness of sins, there is life and salvation.*

MARTIN LUTHER

# 5.

How do you bridge the gap between what a man is and what he ought to be, between what he does and what he ought to do? This is the supreme ethical question. It becomes the supreme religious question. God demands holiness; man is unholy. God demands love; man is unloving. God demands perfection; man is imperfect.

This yawning gap is the focus of man's elemental uneasiness, his deep anxieties, his destructive guilts. It splits his being in two. It drives him to a life of pretense. It makes him a fraud. And it may drive him to despair, as it did Ibsen's Brand, who after a lifetime of trying to fulfill God's law to the letter was completely undone.

How shall a man be justified in the eyes of God? Not by works, says God. For even the most intense effort and the most complete adherence to law will only make man the more aware of the impossible width of the chasm. The Apostle Paul, after such effort, cried, "I do not do the good I want, but the evil I do not want is what I do. . . . Wretched man that I am! Who will deliver me from this body of death?"

There is no bridging the chasm except through *forgiveness,* the overarching forgiveness of God himself. "If thou, Lord, shouldst mark iniquities, O Lord, who shall stand?" cried the Psalmist, and adds, "But there is forgiveness with thee." And forgiveness is the center of the work of Christ on the cross and the doorway to the life abundant.

Among the many ways in which the Bible tells of our Lord's work for us, the forgiveness of sins is central. But there are others. And no comprehension of Christ's salvation would be complete without all the images.

We have the image of the *window*. Christ revealed the heart of God. In and through Christ we understand that God is more than a mighty Sovereign who created the universe and gives it order and precision. We understand that he is more than a lawgiver who holds men to account for their lives and for the management of the planet. In Christ we see a God of infinite compassion and love. We know him as a great and good Father.

We have the image of *warfare*. God wages battle against the enemy and rescues us from his clutches. He invades this earth in his Son, encounters the enemy, and on the cross wins the decisive battle. Christ is the Lord of hosts, the divine warrior. We are now free, not because we wrested ourselves from Satan, but because Christ did it for us. When Napoleon's army went down to defeat in the Russian winter, all the areas in central Europe were suddenly free from the dominion of Napoleon's lieutenants, not because they, in central Europe, achieved victory, but because a decisive defeat occurred hundreds of miles away. Because the enemy went down to defeat nearly 2000 years ago on a little knoll outside the city gates of Jerusalem, at Golgotha, we are free of his demonic rule. We need no longer grovel before him. We can rise up in the victory which was won for us and exult, "Thanks be to God who gives us the victory through our Lord, Jesus Christ."

The profoundest image is still the *court scene*. In this picture the deepest pathos of man's situation is encountered. Man is not only the blind one, needing revelation (the window), nor is he only the defeated one needing victory (the warfare); he is the disobedient one, the rebellious one, needing forgiveness. He need not necessarily feel guilt over not being able to see, nor over not being able to win the victory. He is guilty because, as a free and responsible being, he has disobeyed God. And he must come to terms with his guilt if he is to be whole again.

It is not by accident that the Bible, in Genesis, uses what seems a trifling offense to teach us the nature of obedience and disobedience. Our first parents were told not to eat of the fruit of the tree of knowledge. In their disobedience, Adam and Eve could very well have defended themselves by pleading that their offense after all was a minor one. They had not killed, they had not burned down the garden. They had only tasted of one fruit among many in the garden. Trivial as it seemed, this after all was the one prohibition, the one testing ground for their obedience. The point is, we either obey or we disobey. If we disobey, we are arrayed against God. We are under his judgment, irrespective of the magnitude of the offense.

When we stand before God, we do not sort out the dimensions of obedience and disobedience. We are either obedient or disobedient, we are not guilty, or we are guilty. And there is not a person who stands before God guiltless. We have all sinned and have fallen short.

Nor can we defend ourselves by calculating balances. A bank teller embezzles $1,000 on Monday. Throughout the week, he handles in all $100,000. When arraigned for embezzlement, he defends himself by saying that during the week he handled $99,000 honestly and only $1,000 dishonestly—which should give him a 99-1 balance on the side of honesty. But the one offense made him an embezzler. Whatever balances we may claim, we are sinners—and in need of forgiveness. This is the law of God.

The law's most serious indictment comes at the point of our omissions. In the great judgment scene in Matthew God is pictured as charging men with *not* having done things. "I was hungry and you did not give me to eat. . . . I was a stranger and you did not take me in." There was no question about what they had done. After all, they had not stolen food, they had not evicted anyone. In recent years we have become poignantly aware of the sins of our omissions. We have neglected the hungry of the world; we have stood by to see millions made homeless by the signing of documents in our century; we have overlooked the plight of millions of the dispossessed of our country and of the world. Plead whatever extenuating circumstances we will, our pleas will sound hollow in the ears of God and perhaps in our own ears. We stand in the court, the guilty ones.

If we will indeed repent and turn to God for a fresh chance, his forgiveness will flow over us as a tide. It is there, ever since the cross. It is but waiting for us to let the gates open—the gates of our own broken hearts—and the healing of his pardon will overwhelm us.

His promises are clear. "If any will come, I will in no wise cast him out." "Though your sins be as scarlet, they shall be white as snow." "As far as the east is from the west, so far has he removed our transgressions from us." "There is therefore now no condemnation to them that are in Christ Jesus."

There are people who think this is too easy a religion. Why should men be let off? Why should their guilt be given to another and he take the penalty? Is this not a blatant miscarriage of justice? Is it not basically indecent for God to handle his children in such a casual way?

It certainly is not casual. Picture the court scene. I come, the convicted one and the sentenced one. "The wages of sin is death." I stand there, totally undone. Then the wonder of wonders: the judge steps down from the bench, takes my penalty upon himself, goes to his death for me. I stand in the sight of the court, freed, as if I had never sinned. I am acquitted. The innocence and righteousness of the judge himself are transferred to me. I stand, bewildered—and overcome.

And I am shaken to the depths. Any sentence, even a reduced and merciful one, could not have moved me. But this! What can I say? What can I do? I am free! Free from judgment altogether. And all because a judge who had every right to sentence me to death had such love for me that he went to death himself.

This is the staggering turn of events as I face God. He was in Christ, at the cross, reconciling me and the world to himself. "For God so loved the world that he gave . . ."

I realize now that I am unbelievably the loved one, the forgiven one. I stand before God and the universe as a new man. I have the right to be with the holy God, because I have his holiness. I am without sin, as he is. All because Christ gave me his sinlessness. I am an heir, a joint heir with him, to the vast resources of the kingdom of God.

Who can say that this is a casual way for God to deal with men? It is the most explosive thing that can happen to men—this radical mercy of God.

One of the saddest turns of events in our day is that the church neglects to offer men this magnificent story of forgiveness. We are caught up in the permissiveness of our day. We are intrigued by contextual ethics. We are beguiled by the term *mores* instead of law. We capitulate to the idea that environment and heredity tell the whole story of man. We are skittish about arraigning man before God for judgment. In consequence, we have little to say about forgiveness.

Whether the climate of the times seems to make the message of forgiveness credible or not, we have no option but to declare it. It is the only genius we have as a Christian church. Moreover, there is ample reason to believe that the message may get a more joyous ear than ever. When has fiction, drama, psychiatry ever spoken so generally about the sense of guilt and its pervasiveness? It is the one common denominator which the therapists of the spirit of man recognize. We are a guilt-ridden generation.

And what cure is there for guilt—other than forgiveness, and above all the overarching, comprehensive forgiveness of God? What chance is there for ridding the past of its debris and giving man the right to a fresh start—other than the forgiveness of God?

This is a great hour for the church if it will be

sensitive and bold, sensitive to the tormenting gap which plagues men, and bold to declare the glorious fact of forgiveness of sins in Christ Jesus, our Lord.

Certainly we need to summon the church to the tasks which forgiven men and women have in our time. Forgiveness cries out for action. The forgiven one has the built-in imperative of the gospel to thank him who forgives. And he directs us to our brothers. There is no other channel open for us to thank him. We are to love and to forgive, as we have been and are loved and forgiven.

But the church will be faithless to its primeval purpose if it does not keep proclaiming, in season and out, the wonderful story of God's forgiveness. For this is the only message that can produce loving and forgiving people.

# The Recovery of Hope

*I pray that the God of our Lord Jesus
Christ, the all-glorious Father, may give
you the spiritual powers of wisdom and
vision, by which there comes the
knowledge of him. I pray that your
inward eyes may be illumined, so that
you may know what is the hope to which
he calls you, what the wealth and glory
of the share he offers you among his
people in their heritage, and how vast the
resources of his power open to us who
trust in him.*

Ephesians 1:17-19 (NEB)

# 6.

Hope is the casualty of our day. An avalanche of enormous problems rolls toward us, and we have all but given up on the tomorrows. The future is now, we cry.

This century opened with glowing optimism, at least in this Western world. There had been no major wars. Bismarck had consolidated central Europe without bloodshed. Science had made spectacular gains. Nineteenth-century Enlightenment had inspired extravagant hope in the essential goodness of man and the powers of reason. Horace Mann had predicted that if all men were educated, we could close the prisons. And in the wake of Darwin's *Origin of Species* both philosophers and theologians interpreted life as an irresistible spiral upward and onward to better things. Man was moving from the beast to the angel, carried onward by some force in history itself. It was a great day for the unreflective optimist. That day is now gone.

We are now back to biblical realism. After all, the Bible never pictured man as essentially good, nor does it pin the hope for man on his reason alone. Nor does the Bible describe man as caught in an automatic spiral that will sweep him on to some utopia. The Bible portrays man in perpetual crisis.

The powers of God and the powers of Satan are at

war for man and his world. And man must choose. He cannot abdicate responsibility, rest back, and ride the crest to the better day. If he abdicates, he plunges on to destruction. His will is trapped by deep-seated selfishness which unleashes centrifugal forces that destroy the world. Alone, without God, his most noble efforts will betray him.

It is left to the church alone among all the institutions of society to introduce God into the plight of man, and to put man on the path of hope again. Hope is never easy to come by at best, and the task of the church will call on its most faithful and courageous witness in this dark hour—if it is to recover hope for our distressed age. There will be times when even we who profess the faith feel that we are "whistling in the dark." But God is the God of hope, and we must present him.

We may be tempted to let the world go and simply call attention to the hope for a future on the other side of death. When Ralph Waldo Emerson's maid returned from having heard a street preacher announce that the world was coming to its end in two weeks, and in her panic asked Mr. Emerson, "What shall we do?" he replied, "Don't be so distraught. If it becomes necessary I think we can get along without this world." Yes, indeed. The Christian faith has always included in its future the consummation of a kingdom beyond death and beyond the planet.

But we would not be fair to God if we did not take him seriously on this side of death. This is his world. He has put us here. He has created the planet for our care and our enjoyment. In Christ he has established his kingdom among us. He has much at stake in our future, here and now. And he is on hand to help us realize as fully as possible the life that is here. In his own good time he will introduce the new heaven and the new earth, but until that day he is involved "up to his ears" with our tenure on the earth.

In any recovery of hope, our first step is to take a good hard look at God, rather than to take an inventory of our own ingenuity.

The Old Testament people, then and now, in facing the present and the future, keep looking back to what God has done. The Passover Feast recalls how God delivered his people from the bondage of the Egyptians. If he delivered them then, he can and will deliver them now, and will continue to do so in the future. Any hope for tomorrow will rest in the facts of yesterday. The church lives in memory!

In the Christian church the memory focuses on a cross. That God would so love this world as to send his only son to redeem it—this, above all, is the guarantee of his everlasting love. If he would go to such lengths, what further steps will he not take? He who bought us with such extravagant price cannot let us go.

It is doubtful that men can marshall any confidence

in the future without resting securely in the faith that God is at hand. After all, man was created to be a dependent being. He was never intended to go it alone. Whatever sense of security he may devise for himself, he will always be haunted by his elemental incompetence. He cannot keep his heart beating on his own; he cannot keep the sun shining; he cannot keep his brain from slipping cogs; he has no security against cancer. On countless fronts he faces insecurity. Neither wealth nor station nor even skills can keep him safe. Deep down, he yearns to lean on someone who has the love and resources to see him through.

This is precisely the prayer Paul utters for the people in Ephesus: "I pray . . . that you may know what is the hope to which he calls you, what the wealth and glory of the share he offers you among his people in their heritage, and how vast the resources of his power open to us who trust in him."

The elemental motif for hope is therefore a "resting back" into the love and power of God. This is not to immobilize man for his own efforts. Rather, it is to free him from the fear and the paralysis that he is threatened with on his own. Now, because God is at his side, now he can take heart and go to work. In fact, God puts him to work. He commissions him to take charge of the planet, for him and with him. Man becomes a kind of co-pilot, with the pilot at his side.

Paul poses the question, "If God be for us, who can

be against us?" After all, if God is at work, who are we to set limits on what can happen? With him all things are possible. The future is open. The limitless and unpredictable resources of God are at hand.

This does not allow us to relax our efforts, however. He will call us to account. We are responsible for history. We who claim the comfort of God, who call ourselves followers of Christ, must work harder, think harder, and be involved more deeply than any other. We cannot spurn the disciplines of knowledge. We must call into play all the skills and shrewdness of the social scientist. We must welcome all the ingenuity of technology. Everything must be marshalled to do the will of God for this earth.

Crises may very well be the doors which God is opening for us. Change is not necessarily bad. Old forms may need to go. The new wine of God may strain the old skins to their breaking. The thunder may be the noise of frozen forms breaking up. Winter may be giving way to spring.

In all honesty, are there no signs that may tell of hope? Hope for our grandchildren on the earth? While God may be working in mysterious ways, not easily distinguished, it is not wrong for us to try to see glimmers of light.

The very technology which has unleashed powers that may destroy us may, redirected, be God's gift for making life much better on the earth. It is difficult to believe that he does not approve the great strides that science has made. It is as if the Creator had hidden great prizes in his warehouse, had given men the ingenuity and the curiosity to uncover them, and stands by to applaud every new discovery.

A scientist friend of mine described to me the incredible sources of power now within reach. His eyes shone as he predicted that the time would come when with this power we would convert all the salt water we needed into fresh water, pump it through conduits to any part of the world. The Sahara Desert would bloom like the rose. The arid regions of Asia would be gardens. There would be food, more than enough for everyone.

And are we to deplore the possibilities that seem to loom ahead in the biological sciences? There will be profound ethical issues to face as we can control the formation of human life. But if there have been gains in the control of other kinds of life—crops, for instance—can we not believe that as man's scope of management is enlarged, we may be given wisdom from God to be proper caretakers of increased responsibilities?

Turbulent as our day is with the accelerated pace of change, are there not signs that should hearten us? We yet have a long way to go in social justice, but the past decade has evidenced great gains. At no time in our history have the "haves" been so sensitive to the "have-nots." Never before has the older generation given ear to the younger generation as now, and their voices may be the prophetic ones. In our country concern for the Gross National Product is giving way to a concern for people. And is there not growing, not only in our country but throughout the world, a profound distrust of war as any viable solution to national differences?

And how about interest in the inner man, in religion, in the spiritual dimension of life? Sorokin, in his *The Crisis of Our Age,* says that the sensate age, which began with the Renaissance's emphasis on man as a child of nature, has nearly run its course, and that we are on the threshold of an era when man will understand himself and his needs in terms of his "spirit." That man does not live by bread alone, by the abundance of things, is already far more an awareness in our society than it was even two decades ago. The institutional church may suffer the general disenchantment which the establishment everywhere suffers at the moment, but the message it may have to give about God and the meaning of life will have a more ready ear today than a generation ago.

There are signs of hope, perhaps faint ones, but signs nonetheless. And are we not to have faith that God may indeed be working toward a future on earth more glorious than any we have known?

We are in crisis, to be sure. Tragedy on a colossal

scale could overtake us. But even this does not rob us of a future. The epic character of the Bible's account of God and man has made provision for tragedy and death, even the death of the planet. After all, this earth is only one island in the vast archipelago of our God. When death overtakes us, and can do no more, he who raised Jesus Christ from the dead, will put us on our feet again in another part of his vast empire, to serve him and to enjoy him forever.

In the meantime, however, the only place we can serve him is here and now. The earth is the Lord's, we are the Lord's, and the earth is ours to care for. With him at our side it is for us to let him give of his wisdom and power—and plunge ahead to care for the earth and for our brothers.

# A Style of Life

*Every one then who hears these words of mine and does them will be like a wise man who built his house upon the rock; and the rain fell, and the floods came, and the winds blew and beat upon that house, but it did not fall, because it had been founded on the rock.*

Matthew 7:24-25 (RSV)

# 7.

Does it make any difference? I confess that I believe in God, the Father, Son, and Holy Spirit. So what?

Beliefs matter. They may sprout wings and fly off with you. In fact, they should—if they really are beliefs. "As a man thinketh in his heart, so is he," said the psalmist. Your style of life becomes the outward expression of your faith.

The church is often called "the fellowship of believers." They are a people who confess a faith, and in consequence have a certain style of life. And often their manner of life becomes a more eloquent witness than their confession of faith. It is also possible that their confession may be annulled by their way of life. Emerson said, "I cannot hear what you say, for what you are thunders in my ears."

When someone says that the Christian church has failed, this much is true: it has never lived up to its confession. To this extent it has failed. The precepts of its faith and the exalted style of life of its Lord are simply beyond human achievement. Failure to achieve them, however, is no shame. It would be a shame if its goals were low enough to guarantee success.

To the credit of the church and its Lord, it must be said by any reasonable historian that more good has come into this world by the "unsuccessful" achievements of the followers of Jesus than through any other institution. The style of life which has captured millions of followers down through the centuries has had a revolutionary effect on homes, on governments, on education, on industries. Of the early Christians it was observed, "See how they love one another," and "they are turning the world upside down." They were not perfect to be sure; they often fell short of the noble ways of their Master. But they have made a vast difference in the world. Their beliefs have mattered!

Rather than deny their Lord and conform their lives to something less than the faith they confessed, thousands have gone to their deaths as martyrs, and hundreds of thousands have lived lives of sacrifice and suffering. It is in their company that we today find ourselves as people who confess Jesus Christ as Lord and Savior.

The Holy Spirit is still at work. Through the quiet and commonplace ministry of Word and Sacrament, the Spirit is nudging and guiding the hearts and wills of men. Miracles of change happen. They may not be spectacular; they may be slow and gradual. The clue to this style of life is described in a few short words by Paul in his letter to the Galatians: love, joy, peace, longsuffering, gentleness, goodness, faith, meekness, self-control. If you were able to find the constellation of these qualities in any person, or even fragments of these virtues, could you do other than applaud them as a miracle, the work of the Spirit of God?

Let us examine some of these qualities, especially as reflected in the life of our Lord, and let us do a bit of self-examination. After all, these are the virtues we have a right to claim from the Lord whom we confess.

Love itself is the comprehensive quality. As described in the 13th chapter of First Corinthians, it includes all the others. It is an expansive, unconditioned, and inclusive love. It gives and gives and gives, and never asks. As a great waterfall, pouring its floods year after year, whether anyone thinks to harness its power or not, so is this kind of love. It wells up from within the heart that has received the love of God and keeps lavishing itself upon others, whether people are thankful or not, whether they respond or not, whether anything is achieved or not.

The genius of this love is that its primary object is God himself. Its headwaters are the cross. Because God has so loved me, I want to do something for him. And he deflects me. He takes the love I want to give to him and "fastens" it on my neighbor. I may initially resent this. Suppose I were to be extravagant and give my wife a gift of pearls, only to discover later that she had pawned the gift to help a needy neighbor. What was worse, I did not like this neighbor. Would I not have a right to be resentful? This is the "trick" the Lord plays upon us. He says, "Love me, love the neighbor." The neighbor becomes God's proxy. "Whatever you do for these, you have done for me," he says. He gives us no other channel for the love we would give him.

This puts a totally new light on the business of loving other people. Without this, love can very well become sentiment, a sort of emotional response to people we like or to people who elicit our sympathy and pity. And this is not the sturdy love which the Bible describes.

The love which Jesus Christ lived has built into it almost everything which gives nobility to life.

It has *patience.* It is longsuffering. It knows how to wait. Kipling in his "If" says "If you can wait and not be tired by waiting . . . you'll be a man, my son." How difficult it is to hang on, to keep loving, when nothing seems to happen.

It has *gentleness.* It is sensitive to others, with a sort of sixth sense. It projects itself into the sorrows, the anguish, the fears of others. It does not use an ax to open doors; it waits to use a key.

And it has *imagination.* It has the capacity to be indignant, with a divine anger, over the circumstances which damage people. The battles for justice in our society, carried on with even a touch of ruthlessness, may be inspired by love. Evil must often be crushed. Love can easily reach the limits of tolerance.

It has *joy.* It revels in the greatness and the goodness

of God. It accepts with gratitude and exuberance the beauties of nature, the laughter of a child, the touch of a beloved's hand. After all, there is a sense in which when Christ restored us to the Father, he restored us to the Father's world. And he restored us to our brothers to love and to enjoy. It may very well be that I should seek to enjoy people, rather than to change them. They are God's children and my brothers.

It has *peace*. The heart comes to rest in the love of God. Separation and estrangement are gone. Sins are forgiven and forgotten. Each day is a new day. The peace of the inner man, the peace that God and not the world can give, seeks ways and means to have peace be a way of life between people and between nations. Reconciliation with God pushes out to find reconciliation among all people everywhere.

It has *self-control*. Love is not undisciplined. It is of course an exuberant, spontaneous flow from the heart of God. But man struggles against his baser nature. The devil, the world, and his own sinful self are arrayed against this flow. These wicked powers and impulses must be kept in check. They must be subdued by wise discipline to allow the streams of God's love to have passage.

And it has *expectations*. "Love beareth all things, believeth all things, hopeth all things, endureth all things." It will love to the end. It may be disappointed with the response. But who knows when and how the seed that is sown may sprout? Who knows when a loving act may bear fruit? "Love never fails!" An act of love is caught up in the rivers of God, and they flow into eternity.

The inventory could include many more facets. Love is an organ with many pipes, each adding its tone to the rich, full music of the Christian life. At best, we will only approximate the superb style that the fulness of love dictates. But even an approximation is a glorious thing. Failure lies not in reaching a point less than the mountain's top; failure is not climbing at all.

Whatever excellence of life a person or church may reach, they themselves will be more aware of their shortcomings than of their successes. They will fall back, again and again, on the forgiveness that the Lord has for them. They will live in the wonder of being loved. God's mercy will be their very life. They will scarcely be aware of the loving qualities that God may be producing in them. This unawareness is their charm. To love and to forgive will be a sort of luxury, the high privilege they have as partners in life with God.

There will be a deep, pervasive joy, which even the hard stretches of the road cannot destroy. They will remember their Lord, "who for the joy that was set before him endured the cross." They too, as his followers, will keep on, whatever the odds. I like the story of the coast guard, stationed to help ships in distress. One night a fierce storm was raging. A ship was floundering in the reefs. The captain ordered the rescue boat out. The first mate said, "Captain, it's insane to go out. The gale is off shore; the reefs are terribly treacherous. We could get out there, but we would never get back." The captain said, "Launch the boat. We don't have to get back. We've got to go out!"

We don't have to win. We don't have to save the world. We only have to stay in character as disciples of our Lord, as those who already in him have the ultimate victory secure in our hands. And because we keep on, trying and trying, in and with the unsuspecting resources of God, who knows what ships may indeed be rescued? Who knows what glorious outcome he may yet have for our world?

A congregation is more than meets the eye. We are part of a larger constellation. Surrounding us are the celestial bleachers filled with the saints now released from tragedy and death. Braced by this "great cloud of witnesses" cheering us on, we press on in our high calling as children of God. We too, as they before us, are spurred on by the desire for a city that has everlasting foundations, whose maker and builder is God.

We know that, come what may, the victory is in the hands of our Lord and King. In one of the great galleries there is a picture of the devil playing chess with a man. The title of the picture is "Checkmate," with the devil leering at the man whom he now had defeated. One day an old man entered the hall, stood for a long time gazing at the picture. Suddenly, the corridor rang with his voice, "It's not true; the king has another move."

Our King will always have another move. This is the confidence that undergirds the life of the church of Jesus Christ.